F U N W I

Colors

ALADDIN BOOKS
MACMILLAN PUBLISHING COMPANY   NEW YORK
MAXWELL MACMILLAN CANADA   TORONTO
MAXWELL MACMILLAN INTERNATIONAL
NEW YORK   OXFORD   SINGAPORE   SYDNEY

Red!

RED apples are
crunchy!

What color is this rattle?

Blue!

These BLUE rattles make lots of noise!

What color is this popsicle?

Green!

GREEN popsicles are
sticky and sweet!

What color is this birdie?

Yellow!

These YELLOW birdies
are fun to play with!

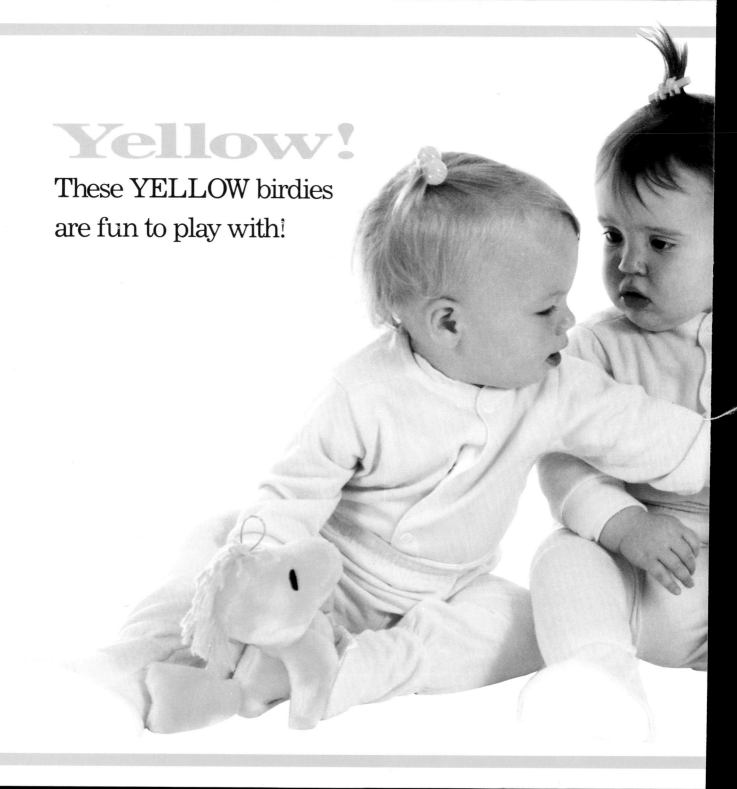

What color is this potato?

Brown!

This BROWN potato sack

holds a baby!

What color is this pumpkin?

Orange!

ORANGE pumpkins
are for Halloween!

What color is this bunny?

Gray!

GRAY bunnies are cute and cuddly!

What color is this feather?

Purple!

PURPLE feathers can tickle!

What color is this teddy bear?

Pink!

PINK teddy bears
are soft and fuzzy!

What color is this hat?

Black!

Big BLACK hats
are fun to wear!